Ac...ystem

Rod Theodorou

Heinemann
LIBRARY

www.heinemann.co.uk/library
Visit our website to find out more information about Heinemann Library books.

To order:
☎ Phone 44 (0) 1865 888112
🗎 Send a fax to 44 (0) 1865 314091
🖳 Visit the Heinemann bookshop at www.heinemann.co.uk/library to browse our catalogue and order online.

First published in Great Britain by Heinemann Library, Halley Court, Jordan Hill, Oxford OX2 8EJ, part of Harcourt Education.
Heinemann is a registered trademark of Harcourt Education Ltd.

Editorial: Clare Lewis
Design: Victoria Bevan, Michelle Lisseter, and Bridge Creative Services
Illustrations: Stephen Lings and Jane Pickering at Linden Artists
Picture Research: Hannah Taylor
Production: Helen McCreath

Printed in China

13 digit ISBN 978 0 431 05654 8 (hardback)
10 09 08 07 06
10 9 8 7 6 5 4 3 2 1

13 digit ISBN 978 0 431 05765 1 (paperback)
11 10 09 08 07
10 9 8 7 6 5 4 3 2 1

British Library Cataloguing in Publication Data
Theodorou, Rod and Telford, Carole
Amazing journeys: Across the Solar System – 2nd edition
577.7'89
A full catalogue record for this book is available from the British Library.

Acknowledgements
The publishers would like to thank the following for permission to reproduce photographs:
Corbis/epa/NASA p. 27; Oxford Scientific Films: NASA pp. **16**, **17**; Science Photo Library: European Space Agency p. **10**; Ludek Pesek p. **23**; Mehau Kulyk p. **11**; NASA pp. **13**, **14**, **15**, **17**, **19**, **20**, **21**, **22**, **24**, **25**, **26**; National Optical Astronomy Observatories p. **11**; US Geological Survey pp. **12**, **18**; Victor Habbick Visions p. **6**.

Cover artwork of the Solar System, reproduced with permission of Science Photo Library/ Detlev Van Ravenswaay.

The publishers would like to thank Nick Sample for his assistance in the preparation of this book.

Every effort has been made to contact copyright holders of any material reproduced in this book. Any omissions will be rectified in subsequent printings if notice is given to the publishers.

The paper used to print this book comes from sustainable resources.

Contents

Introduction   6

Journey map   8

The blazing Sun   10

Mercury: the dead world   12

Venus: our savage sister   14

Earth: the water planet   16

Mars: the red planet   18

Jupiter: gas giant   20

Saturn: the ringed planet   22

Uranus: the green planet   24

Neptune: the blue planet   **25**

Pluto: mystery planet   **26**

Exploring space: planet probe   **27**

Glossary   **28**

Space calendar   **30**

Find out more   **31**

Index   **32**

Some words are shown in bold, **like this**. You can find out what these words mean by looking in the Glossary.

Introduction

You are about to go on an amazing journey. You are going to climb inside a spaceship, more advanced than any that exists today. You are going to travel to the centre of our **Solar System**, across millions of kilometres, to witness the blazing fury of our spectacular Sun. Then you are going to travel away from the Sun, across silent, cold, black space. You are going to visit each of our Solar System's nine planets, from the dead, colourless world of Mercury, to the dazzling, rainbow storm-clouds of Jupiter.

As you visit each planet you will learn how very different they are and how precious our own planet is – the only planet in the Solar System that can support millions of life forms.

1	Sun
2	Mercury
3	Venus
4	Earth
5	Mars
6	Jupiter
7	Saturn
8	Uranus
9	Neptune
10	Pluto

The first four "inner" planets are small rocky worlds. Four of the "outer" planets are "gas giants" – huge balls of gases and liquids. Pluto is the smallest and furthest planet from the Sun.

Outer planets

Inner planets

All the planets in our Solar System move around the Sun ("solar" means "of the Sun"). The Sun is a massive ball of exploding gases called a **star**. There are billions of other stars in our **galaxy**. Many of them also have planets **orbiting** in their own solar systems.

Our spaceship is designed to travel at incredible speed. Its **hull** can withstand crushing **pressures** as well as intense heat and cold. We are going to need it, because we are going to explore places that have never been set foot on before. What will they be like? Could they support other forms of life?

The spaceship's engines fire up. You are about to find out.

1	Sun
2	Mercury
3	Venus
4	Earth
5	Mars
6	Jupiter
7	Saturn
8	Uranus
9	Neptune
10	Pluto

The planets move around the sun in an **oval** path called an orbit. Our Earth orbits the Sun just like any other planet. Our Earth year is the time it takes to orbit the Sun once.

Journey map

Here is a map of our space journey. We head straight for the Sun, and go as near as we can before turning and heading out towards the planets. On our way we will see many huge lumps of rock and metal tumbling through space. These **asteroids orbit** the Sun just like the planets. We may also see **comets**. Comets are like huge, dirty icebergs, shooting through space. As they break up and melt they leave a "tail" of gas and dust behind them, millions of kilometres long. As we visit some planets we will also see their moons. Moons are huge balls of rock and ice that orbit around some planets.

Mars

Earth

Mercury

Page 18

Page 10

Venus

Page 12

Page 16

Page 14

Comet

Sun

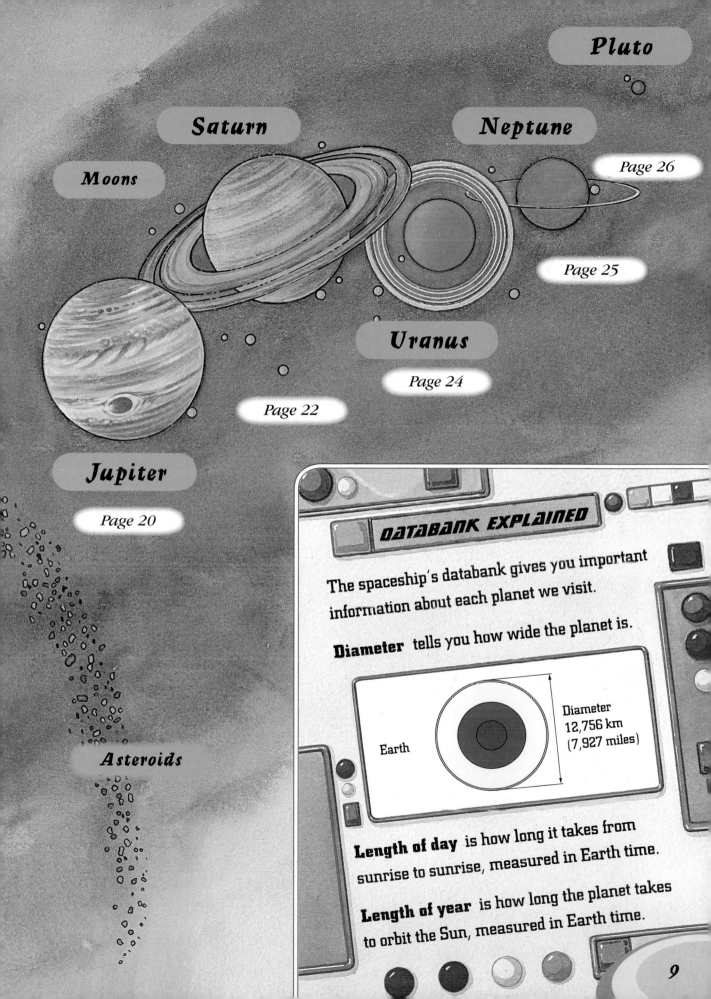

Pluto

Saturn

Moons

Neptune

Page 26

Page 25

Uranus

Page 24

Page 22

Jupiter

Page 20

Asteroids

DATABANK EXPLAINED

The spaceship's databank gives you important information about each planet we visit.

Diameter tells you how wide the planet is.

Earth

Diameter
12,756 km
(7,927 miles)

Length of day is how long it takes from sunrise to sunrise, measured in Earth time.

Length of year is how long the planet takes to orbit the Sun, measured in Earth time.

The blazing Sun

Our spaceship crosses 150 million kilometres (93 million miles) in just a few minutes. Temperature **gauges** go higher and higher as we approach the centre of our **Solar System** – the Sun. It is vast – one million times bigger than the Earth! It fills our **protective** screens until all we can see is red fire.

The Sun is like an immense **nuclear** explosion. Its surface is a bubbling, boiling mass of burning gases. It has been burning for five billion years. In another six billion years it will grow in size to become an even bigger flaming ball, called a red giant. When this happens, the Earth and all life in our Solar System will be destroyed.

Without the Sun's warmth, there would be no life on Earth. Plants use the Sun's **energy** to grow. Without plants, animals would have nothing to feed on.

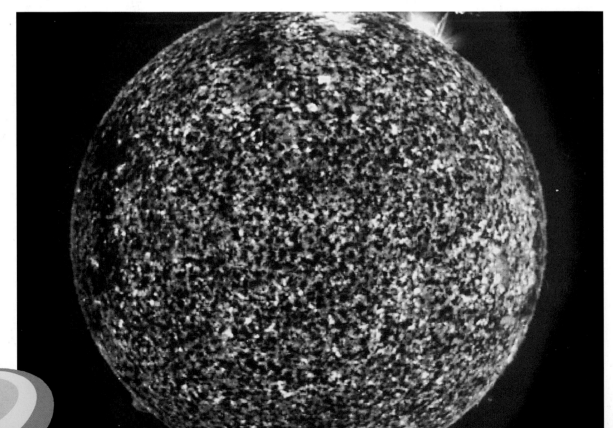

DATABANK

Distance from the Earth — 150 million kilometres (93 million miles)

Diameter — 1,392,530 kilometres (865,318 miles)

Size comparison

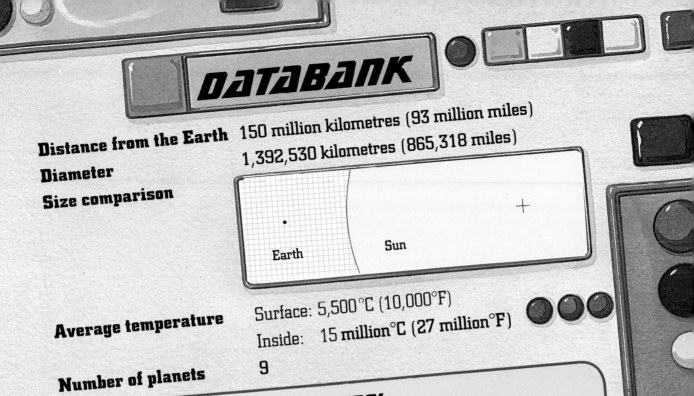

Earth · Sun +

Average temperature — Surface: 5,500°C (10,000°F)
Inside: 15 million°C (27 million°F)

Number of planets — 9

WARNING!

This spaceship is fitted with protective screens.
Looking directly at the Sun is dangerous. Never look at the
Sun through **binoculars** or a **telescope** – it can blind you!

Solar flares

Sometimes immense jets of flame **erupt** from the Sun's surface and shoot out into space.

Sunspots

The Sun appears to have black areas on its surface. These "sunspots" are places where the surface is slightly cooler. Sunspots can be as big as the Earth.

Mercury: the dead world

Touchdown! We have landed on the first of the four "inner" planets. Tiny Mercury is only a one twentieth of the size of the Earth. It is the nearest planet to the Sun. It has almost no blanket of **atmosphere** around it, to protect it from the Sun's rays, or keep the warmth in at night. There is never any gust of wind or drop of rain. There are no clouds or colour in the sky. Even though it is daytime we can see twinkling stars and the huge Sun, which looks three times bigger than from Earth.

A day lasts two Earth months here – two Earth months of searing heat and **radiation**. We are glad our spaceship's **hull** can withstand the heat, which is four times hotter than boiling water. That is hot enough to melt lead! When the night does come, temperatures will drop far beyond freezing point.

Mercury is only slightly bigger than our own Moon. This photo, taken by the Mariner 10 space probe, shows it also looks like our Moon.

Distance from the Sun   58 million kilometres (36 million miles)

Diameter   4,879 kilometres (3,032 miles)

Size comparison

Earth   Mercury

Average temperature   Day: 400 °C (720°F)
Night: -170 °C (-300°F)

Length of day   58·5 Earth days

Length of year   88 Earth days

Number of moons   0

Craters

A crater is the round "scar" left by a **meteorite** smashing into a planet, just like a pebble thrown into sand. Mercury's landscape is blasted with huge craters made by meteorites that showered the planet millions of years ago.

Caloris Basin

These small craters are inside the largest crater in the Solar System. It was caused by a massive **asteroid** hitting Mercury, throwing out crater walls the size of mountains.

Venus: our savage sister

Venus is often called our **twin** or sister planet. Named after the ancient Roman goddess of beauty, it is the closest planet to the Earth, and almost the same size. It is also the brightest planet visible from the Earth. However, there is one thing that makes Venus a very different sister – its **atmosphere**.

Venus has a cloudy atmosphere so thick it presses down on the surface like a million blankets. If we stepped outside our spaceship, we would be crushed as flat as paper. No heat can escape the atmosphere. It is like being trapped inside a huge greenhouse, with temperatures rising even higher than on Mercury. This "greenhouse effect" causes **sulphuric acid** to rain down from the violent raging storms above.

We do not stay long on Venus.

This picture of the surface of Venus is made up of many smaller photographs taken by the Magellan space probe. It spent four years in **orbit** around Venus.

Distance from the Sun 108 million kilometres (67 million miles)
Diameter 12,104 kilometres (7,521 miles)
Size comparison

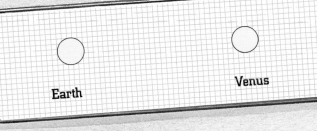

Earth   Venus

Average temperature 480 °C (900°F)
Length of day 243 Earth days
Length of year 224.5 Earth days
Number of moons 0

Visitors to Venus

Four Russian *Venera* space probes have landed on Venus and photographed its surface. It is hot, dry, and quite smooth. Storms and high **pressure** have **eroded** many of the mountains and hills away.

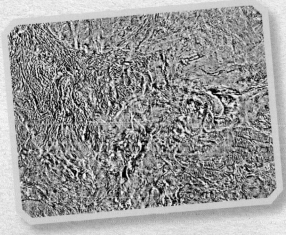

Magellan Probe

In 1989 the *Magellan* probe was launched and in 1990 it sent back photos of Venus. They showed that there may once have been oceans on Venus, but these boiled away millions of years ago.

Earth: the water planet

Our spaceship takes us into an **orbit** around our own planet. As we circle over the Pacific Ocean all we can see is blue water. After the violent acid storms of Venus, the Earth looks gentle and welcoming.

The Earth's **atmosphere** protects its surface like a blanket from the intense heat of the Sun on one side and the coldness of space on the other. If it were much colder, all the water would turn to ice. If it were much hotter, all the water would boil away. Earth is the only planet where the temperature is just right for lots of liquid water. The atmosphere also keeps in plenty of air. It is the warmth of the Sun, and the water and air which make the Earth just the right kind of planet for living things to survive.

White storm clouds swirl above the Earth's surface.

16

DATABANK

Distance from the Sun	150 million kilometres (93 million miles)
Diameter	12,756 kilometres (7,927 miles)
Size comparison	

Earth   Moon

Average temperature	14 °C (57°F)
Length of day	24 hours
Length of year	365.25 days
Number of moons	1

The Moon

The Moon is a dead world, much like Mercury. It has no atmosphere and so has no air, no blue sky, no water, and no weather. It orbits the Earth once every 27.3 days. Twelve people have landed on its surface.

Seas without water

The Moon's surface is heavily cratered from **meteorites** and **asteroids** crashing into its surface. Some of these asteroid collisions were so violent they melted the Moon's surface, flooding it with **lava**. These lava flows left huge dark flat patches which we call "seas".

Mars: the red planet

Our spaceship breaks out of the Earth's **orbit** and crosses millions of kilometres to approach a planet about half the size of the Earth. We land on its surface and soon see why Mars is called the red planet. This cold and dusty planet is covered in red dust. Sometimes the wind whips this up into huge, red sandstorms. In many ways this is the most similar planet to the Earth. It has a thin **atmosphere** and a day lasts almost exactly the same time as on Earth. Out of our **portholes** we see a world quite similar to an Earth desert. The sky is pink with a few wispy clouds. The wind blows across orange sand dunes, craters, huge dead **volcanoes**, and mountains. One of these, Olympus Mons, is the largest volcano in the **Solar System**, three times higher than Mount Everest!

The spectacular surface of Mars, photographed by the *Viking Orbiter*.

DATABANK

Distance from the Sun	228 million kilometres (142 million miles)
Diameter	6,794 kilometres (4,222 miles)
Size comparison	

Earth   Mars

Average temperature	-63 °C (-81°F)
Length of day	24 Earth hours
Length of year	687 Earth days
Number of moons	2

Waterworld

Many scientists believe that millions of years ago Mars was a warmer planet and it had its own seas. Now the water has gone, but we can still see what look like dried up riverbeds. This photo was taken by the *Viking Orbiter*.

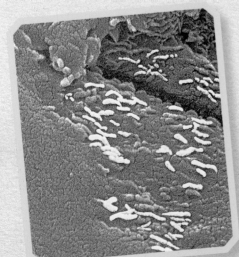

Martians?

In 1984 a **meteorite** that appears to be a lump of rock from Mars landed on Earth. Some scientists think it has tiny **fossils** of **bacteria** on its surface. Could this mean there was once life on Mars?

Jupiter: gas giant

As we get nearer and nearer to Jupiter we can hardly believe its size. It is the largest planet in the **Solar System** – 1,266 times bigger than the Earth. Its surface is beautiful. It looks like white, red, brown, and orange paints, swirling and mixing. A giant red eye on its surface seems to look at us. Our spaceship plunges straight into its churning **atmosphere**. We travel down through thick white and orange clouds, flashing with lightning, then into bluish, icy water droplets, and finally into gases so thick it is almost like being under water. It gets darker and darker. Somewhere beneath us is the rocky **core**. The incredible heat and **pressure** outside are damaging our **hull**. We turn around and head for space.

Jupiter is a giant ball of gases.

Distance from the Sun	778 million kilometres (483 million miles)
Diameter	142,984 kilometres (88,850 miles)
Size comparison	

Earth

Jupiter

Average temperature	-150 °C (-238°F)
Length of day	10 Earth hours
Length of year	12 Earth years
Number of moons	16

The red spot

Jupiter is a planet of incredible storms. The Great Red Spot is the largest storm in the Solar System. This massive **hurricane**, three times wider than the Earth, has been raging for 300 years!

Life on Europa?

Europa is one of Jupiter's many moons. Scientists think there may be a 100-kilometre (62-mile) deep ocean beneath its icy surface. If this ocean also contains underwater **volcanoes**, there may be the water and heat needed to support life.

Saturn: the ringed planet

We are now into deep space, many millions of kilometres from the Earth. A huge and amazing planet fills our viewing screens. Saturn is the second largest of the planets. It is very similar to Jupiter and just as beautiful. Like Jupiter, it is a vast ball of gases with an inner core of rock and

Saturn is covered in hazy yellow clouds.

ice. Around the planet are huge flat rings made from lumps of rock and ice that **orbit** the planet like billions of tiny moons.

We do not enter Saturn's **atmosphere**. Like Jupiter it is a planet of amazing storms. Winds can blow up to 1,800 kilometres (1,120 miles) per hour! Beneath the stormy surface are hundreds of kilometres of thick, heavy gases, ice, and water **vapour**.

Distance from the Sun 1,429 million kilometres (888 million miles)

Diameter 120,536 kilometres (74,901 miles)

Size comparison

Earth   Saturn

Average temperature -180 °C (-292°F)

Length of day 10.5 Earth hours

Length of year 29.5 Earth years

Number of moons 18

Saturn's rings

We do not know exactly how Saturn's rings were made. Some scientists think Saturn pulled lots of space "rubble" into its orbit millions of years ago. Others think a giant **asteroid** may have hit and destroyed a small moon, leaving rings of rubble and ice. Most think they may have been formed like this:

1. A giant asteroid got caught in Saturn's orbit.

2. As it was pulled around the planet it started to break up.

3. The rings are the remains of the asteroid that still orbit the planet.

Uranus: the green planet

Uranus is the third largest planet. As we approach it we can see its 11 rings, but they are not as beautiful as the bright icy rings of Saturn. They are very thin and hard to see because they are made from black lumps of rock and fine black dust. Dense, green-blue gases cover the planet in a thick, cloudy fog. What lies beneath this smoggy layer? Only one **space probe**, *Voyager 2*, has ever flown past this gas giant. We think it is made from thick gases surrounding a rocky core. We dare not risk damage to our spaceship, so we continue our journey.

This is an artist's painting of Uranus, showing the thin rings.

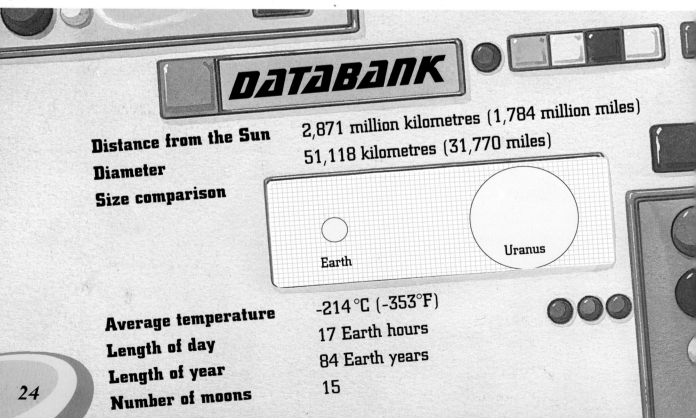

DATABANK

Distance from the Sun	2,871 million kilometres (1,784 million miles)
Diameter	51,118 kilometres (31,770 miles)
Size comparison	Earth · Uranus
Average temperature	-214°C (-353°F)
Length of day	17 Earth hours
Length of year	84 Earth years
Number of moons	15

Neptune: the blue planet

This blue-green planet is similar to Uranus. It is a gas giant and it also has thin dark rings of dust and rock. We are careful not to get too close to Neptune's surface. This is a freezing-cold world with violent storms as big as the Earth! Winds here can travel at incredible speeds, up to 2,000 kilometres (1,240 miles) per hour – the fastest in the **Solar System**. We see a streak of wispy clouds known as the "scooter" which travels completely around the giant planet every 16 hours!

It is easy to see why Neptune was named after the Roman god of the sea.

DATABANK

Distance from the Sun	4,504 million kilometres (2,798 million miles)
Diameter	49,528 kilometres (30,777 miles)
Size comparison	Earth Neptune
Average temperature	-220 °C (364°F)
Length of day	19 Earth hours
Length of year	165 Earth years
Number of moons	8

Pluto: mystery planet

Far away in the distance we can see Pluto, the furthest of the **Solar System's** planets from the Sun. It is a tiny planet, smaller than our own Moon. It is so far away even the most powerful **telescopes** cannot discover much about its surface. We know it must be a very cold planet, covered in layers of ice and frozen gases. Some scientists think Pluto may not even be a true planet. It may simply be a large **comet**. Warning signs flash in our spaceship. Unless we turn around now we will not have enough fuel to get back to Earth. Pluto will have to remain a mystery. It is time to go home.

Pluto is too far away for us to photograph in any detail.

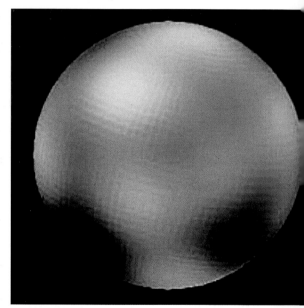

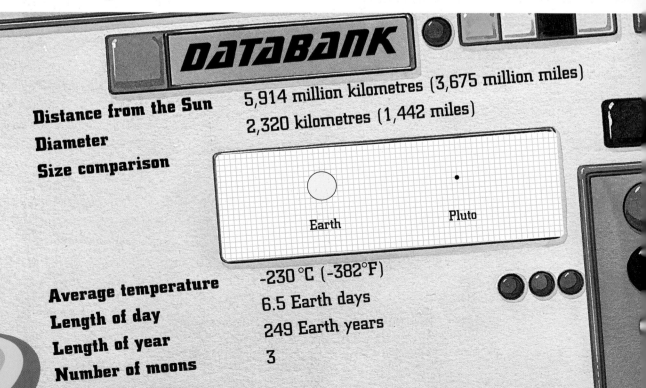

DATABANK

Distance from the Sun	5,914 million kilometres (3,675 million miles)
Diameter	2,320 kilometres (1,442 miles)
Size comparison	Earth Pluto
Average temperature	-230 °C (-382°F)
Length of day	6.5 Earth days
Length of year	249 Earth years
Number of moons	3

Exploring space: planet probe

Of course the spaceship we travelled in in this book does not yet exist. All the information comes from what we have discovered from **telescopes** and **space probes**. Some of the space probes sent into space simply **orbit** planets, sending pictures and other information back to Earth by radio signals. Others are built to enter a planet's **atmosphere** and even land on the surface. The picture on the right shows how one probe, *Sojourner*, visited Mars in 1997. The planets are so far away it would take a lot of money and time to build a spaceship that could visit even the closest of them (Mars). For the moment, scientists are building space stations to orbit the Earth. These tell us more about how to live in space. Perhaps it is only a matter of time before humans can make amazing journeys across the Solar System.

The Mars Exploration Rover set off for Mars in 2003.

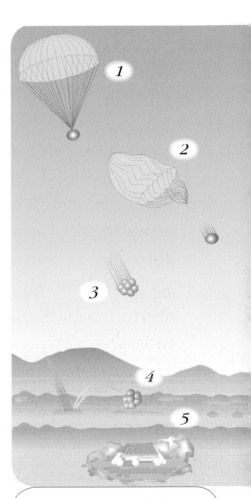

1 *The* Mars Pathfinder *pod parachutes down to the surface of Mars.*
2 *The parachutes are released.*
3 *Large balloons inflate around the pod.*
4 *The pod bounces down on the surface.*
5 *The pod opens to release* Sojourner.

Glossary

asteroid   small planet, less than 500 kilometres (310 miles) wide, found in a belt between Mars and Jupiter in our Solar System

astronaut   person who is trained to work and travel in a spacecraft

atmosphere   the mixture of gases around the Earth, a star or a planet

bacteria   tiny organisms that live in the soil, in water, in the bodies of animals and plants, and can be helpful or harmful

binoculars   instrument with lenses for both eyes, used to make faraway objects look nearer and clearer

comet   object in space made from gas, dust, and ice which travels around the Sun in an orbit

core   the centre of something

cosmonaut   a Russian astronaut

energy   having the ability to work or be active

erode   to wear away

erupt   to explode or shoot out material such as lava and rock

fossil   the remains of a living thing, saved in or turned into rock

galaxy   one of the millions of enormous collections of stars, other Solar Systems, dust, and gases that make up space

gauge   instrument for measuring or testing something

hull   the frame of a ship

hurricane   a very strong wind of at least 120 kilometres (75 miles) per hour

lava   hot, melting rock that comes out of an erupting volcano or cracks in a planet or moon's surface

meteorite	small, solid object that falls from space and hits a planet with incredible impact
nuclear	something related to or powered by nuclear energy
orbit	the path of a planet or satellite around another object in space
oval	egg-shaped
porthole	window in the side of a ship
pressure	the weight of something pressing or being pressed
protective	something that is designed to look after you or shield you
radiation	when energy is sent out in strong rays
satellite	something that moves around another, bigger object
Solar System	the nine planets, and the comets and asteroids that orbit around the Sun
space probe	spacecraft that sends information back to Earth about space
star	a large object such as the Sun, that is very hot and makes its own energy by nuclear reactions
sulphuric acid	a thick, colourless, oily liquid which is a dangerous acid made from sulphur
telescope	an instrument, with only one lens to look through, that makes distant objects seem nearer and larger
twin	one of a pair of identical or similar things
vapour	gas, like mist, that occurs when some substances are heated
volcanoes	a hole or crack in the Earth's crust through which lava, hot gases, rocks, and ash sometimes explode

Space calendar

October 1957	The Soviet Union launches Sputnik 1, the first man-made **satellite** to orbit the Earth.
April 1961	Yuri Gagarin becomes the first human to fly into space.
June 1963	**Cosmonaut** Valentina Tereshkova becomes the first woman in space.
July 1969	*Apollo 11* lands on the Moon. On 21 July Neil Armstrong is the first human to walk on the Moon.
May 1971	The Soviet space probe *Mars 3* lands on Mars.
October 1975	The Soviet probe *Venera 9* lands on Venus.
April 1981	The first Space Shuttle, *Columbia*, is launched into space.
July 1997	NASA's *Pathfinder* visits Mars and *Sojourner* sends back photographs from the surface.
April 2001	The world's first space tourist takes a trip into space. Dennis Tito pays $20 million for his voyage to the International Space Station.
January 2004	Two buggies, *Spirit* and *Opportunity* land on Mars.
March 2004	Astronomers discover a new planet-like asteroid orbiting the Sun. They nickname it Sedna.
July 2005	Astronomers discover another planet-like object. They nickname it Xena. Some scientists think it is an asteroid. But Xena is bigger than Pluto and orbits the Sun. Could this be the 10th planet?
January 2006	A spacecraft called *New Horizons* is launched on a mission to Pluto and beyond.

Find out more

Further reading

DK Guide to Space, Peter Bond
(Dorling Kindersley, 2004)

*Is There Life on Other Planets?:
The Planets of our Solar System*
(Heinemann Library, 2006)

Solar System (Young Knowledge),
Mike Goldsmith (Kingfisher, 2004)

Organizations

British Astronomical Association

Burlington House
Piccadilly
London W1V 0DU
www.britastro.org

Institute of Astronomy

University of Cambridge
Madingley Road
Cambridge
CB3 0HA

www.ast.cam.ac.uk

Using the Internet

If you want to find out more about
the Solar System, you can go to
one of these website addresses.
Alternatively, you can use a search
engine, such as www.yahooligans.com
or www.internet4kids.com, and type
in a keyword such as "Solar System",
or a related subject such as "asteroids".

Websites

www.nasa.gov/kids.html

The USA's National Aeronautics and
Space Administration (NASA) has
many Internet sites, including this
one for kids.

www.space.com

This website is packed with the latest
space news and photos.

www.seds.org/billa/tnp/

This "multimedia tour of the Solar
System" describes the history,
mythology, and current scientific
thinking about the planets, moons,
and other objects in the Solar System.

Index

asteroids 8, 9, 13, 17, 23

atmosphere 12, 14, 16, 17, 18, 20

Caloris Basin 13

comets 8, 26

craters 13, 17, 18

day length and year length 12, 13,
    15, 17, 18, 19, 21, 23, 24, 25, 26

Earth 6, 7, 8, 10, 16, 17

energy 10

Europa 21

gases 6, 7, 10, 20, 22, 24, 26

Jupiter 6, 7, 9, 20-1

lava flows 17

life forms 16, 19, 21

Mars 6, 7, 8, 18-19, 27

Mercury 6, 7, 8, 12-13

meteorites 13, 17, 19

Moon 17

moons 8, 9, 19, 21, 23, 24, 25, 26

mountains 15, 18

Neptune 6, 7, 9, 25

Olympus Mons 18

orbit 7, 8, 14, 22, 27

Pluto 6, 7, 9, 26

radiation 12

red giant 10

rings 22, 23, 24, 25

Saturn 6, 7, 9, 22-3

solar flares 11

space probes 12, 14, 15, 18, 19,
    24, 27

space stations 27

stars 7, 12

storms 14, 18, 21, 22, 25

sulphuric acid 14

Sun 6, 7, 8, 10-11, 12

sunspots 11

temperatures 11, 12, 13, 15, 16,
    17, 19, 21, 23, 24, 25, 26

Uranus 6, 7, 9, 24

Venus 6, 7, 8, 14-15

volcanoes 18, 21

water 16, 19, 21, 22